THE BOOK OF
COURAGE

To me courage is a statement of one's character, it requires a self-perpetuating belief that I can make things work and that nothing is impossible. The bravest of us have no limits, at its core: my courage is the desire to outdo myself. The motto games (a place were you stand up in front of the world and try to outperform history) are citius, altius, fortius. Faster, higher, stronger. Simple yet flawless, the epitome of no boundaries, no limits, the only goal is to do your very best. It doesn't mean faster, higher, stronger than anyone else, just faster, higher, stronger.

Stephane Janson

THE BOOK OF
COURAGE

SELECTED, WRITTEN, AND ILLUSTRATED BY
HANS WILHELM

All inquiries should be addressed to:
Barron's Educational Series, Inc.
250 Wireless Boulevard
Hauppauge, New York 11788
www.barronseduc.com

Library of Congress Catalog Card No.: 2006042676

ISBN-13: 978-0-7641-5958-9
ISBN-10: 0-7641-5958-5

Library of Congress Cataloging-in-Publication Data

Wilhelm, Hans, 1945-
   The book of courage / selected, written, and illustrated by Hans Wilhelm.
      p.cm.
   ISBN-13: 978-0-7641-5958-9
   ISBN-10: 0-7641-5958-5
    I. Courage—Quotations, maxims, etc. I. Title.

BJ1533.C8W53 2006
179'.6—dc22

                                                                                  2006042676

Printed in China
9 8 7 6 5 4 3 2

Contents

*As you move through life, set aside good ideas
and give them to others to encourage and inspire.*

Peter J. Daniels

Preface

For the past 40 years I have been studying, writing, and teaching universal laws on the mastery of life. With time the essence of these laws have become powerful tools that have guided and reminded me whenever my own world seemed to turn upside down.

With this book I wish to share with the reader some of the most potent quotations with regard to courage that I have collected over the years. Many come from my own writings and lectures. Some I have gathered from books and teachings that I have studied. Others come from anonymous sources.

I express deep gratitude to all the teachers who have touched my life and who have graciously shared their insights into how to open heart and mind. Furthermore, this book would not have been written without the persistence and encouragement of my friend Penny Cohen, the author of *Personal Kabbalah*. And special thanks goes to my wonderful wife, Judy Henderson, for her unceasing patience, love, and artistic support.

A man of courage
is also full of faith....
Cicero

Introduction

Time for Courage

Stormy days are part of living on this planet. Their main purpose is to wake us up, throw us out of our comfort zones, and force us to reevaluate our priorities. In all likelihood we have all gone through our share of downpours and more or less survived them all. We have learned from these experiences, and in most cases we have become stronger and more confident. As the old saying goes, "If it doesn't break us, it will make us."

But in spite of these experiences, more people than ever before are today worried and afraid. Watching the news on television makes us believe that the future outlook for our world is bleak. Whether it is the accelerating deterioration of our environment, pollution of the air and water, global warming, bankrupt governments, religious and ethnic violence, social unrest, overpopulation, natural disasters, or any other topic, many dark clouds are gathering on the horizon. Some see this as the fulfillment of biblical prophecies. Others call it the Great Shift of global consciousness or go by more popular prophecies like the Mayan calendar, which seems to predict that our present civilization will come to an end by 2012. In any case, the troubling state of our anxious world is a direct result of an old and outdated value system in which everything was divided into "us" and "them," in black and white, in right and wrong. This "us" can be myself, my family, my group, my nation. It is a form of tribalism where the major driving force is the belief in being superior to others by pointing fingers and blaming them with self-righteous cries for justice and revenge. This old paradigm has not worked and needs to be replaced with a new way of thinking and acting if we want to survive individually and collectively. As Albert Einstein is reputed to have said, "The significant problems we have cannot be solved at the same level of consciousness with which we created them." What we now need is a quantum leap to a higher consciousness. This new consciousness has always been in us as our Higher Self (God-Self, Christ consciousness) that knows about the Oneness with all that is and the sacredness of all life. Collectively and individually we have to make this shift. Many will not be ready because initially it requires an awful lot of courage to think, act, and speak according to our Higher Self. But for those who are willing to make this shift I have written this book containing helpful tools to succeed in this exciting transition.

Naturally, there will be lots of obstacles in our way and many temptations to fall back into the old way of thinking and judging—but with courage we will be able to face these challenges. This leads us to the question: What is courage? The root of the word "courage" is the Latin word *cor*, which means "heart." Our English word "core" has the same Latin root. Webster says that "courage implies firmness of mind and will in the face of danger or extreme difficulty." A person with courage is someone who has faith that all necessary strength and energy will be available to him or her in case of need. But it is more than blind faith; it is the faith in ourselves that we will be willing to do the work step by step to reach the goal. Why don't we always have such faith in our own inner powers? The reason is our ego, also often called our "little self," which stands in contrast to our Higher Self. The ego is like a little child: loud, demanding, and controlling most of our daily thinking, acting, and speaking. It lets us believe that we are better and more important or more special than others. But when we look at this ego more closely we see that it consists of nothing but our past memory, and therefore it can only relate to what we know. This is the reason why the ego is so attached to tribalism (group identity), which is past-oriented. The ego is frightened about anything unfamiliar, such as the future or change. It doesn't want us to see our full potentiality and our true identity. After all, we are powerful, radiant Beings created in the image of the Creator! Our ego has invented four very convincing illusions that prevent us from remembering who we really are. To feel courageous and strong in the face of any approaching storm, we sooner or later have to break through these four illusions:

The First Illusion: ***The world we are living in is real***

Our world and the entire material universe are more like a mirage. It is not the ultimate Reality of God—our real Home—but merely its weak reflection. Collectively we are all making it up—like a dream. The Hindus call it Maya, the great illusion or unreality. Sages and prophets have said this for thousands of years. Quantum physicists have now confirmed their ancient wisdom that this world is a mental construct. In her book *The Field,* Lynne McTaggart writes how the latest observation in quantum physics "had shattering implications about the nature of reality. It suggested that the consciousness of the observer brought the observed object into being." This implies that every minute of every day we are creating our world thought by thought. Most importantly, it suggests that we can change this reality, as it is not fixed, but fluid, or mutable. In other words, if we can create this world, we can also change it, too. That's how powerful we are!

The Second Illusion: ***I am all alone***

In our illusionary world we believe our eyes more than our heart. When we look around us we believe we are alone, separate from each other, and in particular, separate from God. That is the illusion. We are all part of God, like members of the

Body of God ("But now are they many members, yet but one body" 1 Cor. 12:20). We cannot be without God and neither can we be away from God because we are all One. Christ confirmed this with his words "The Father and I are One" (John 10:30). That makes everyone who has dedicated his or her life to Christ automatically one with the Father. But so is everybody else, because there is nothing outside of God. God is omnipresent, omnipotent, and omniscient. God is the "Alpha and the Omega," the Sum Total of Everything, the Totality, and we do not stand outside of this. In other words: It's all God. There is nothing but God. God is all there is. God is within us and we are within God. Can we grasp the truth that we are not outside of God but one with God? This is the most powerful truth our ego doesn't want us to remember.

The Third Illusion: *The world is full of victims and villains*

Although this world is an illusion, it still has its own ironclad laws that govern our lives. Everything in the universe occurs in perfect order and by design. There are no accidents and there is no such thing as coincidence. There are only consequences of our thoughts, feelings, words, and actions—also called the Law of Cause and Effect. Jesus taught it with these words: "Whatsoever you sow, so shall you reap." Nothing comes to us that we have not initiated ourselves on this or any other level of consciousness. Everything that is happening to us occurs for our ultimate benefit and growth. Furthermore, the "other" person is not separate from us, and for as long as we blame the other for our situation, we are caught in the game of the ego and we are losing energy. A courageous person does not fall for the illusion of "victimhood." Instead of being stuck in the past or blaming the past, a courageous person will ask: What can I do *now*?

The Fourth Illusion: *There are shortcuts back to Heaven*

The human language does not have words that could even begin to describe the Ultimate Reality of God—our true Home. Therefore, we are using symbols, such as

Life, Light, and most of all, Love. But this Love is not the same as romantic love. God or God's Love is unlimited, unconditional, and all-inclusive. For us to "wake up" or to return back to the Source, our Home, we would need to be of the same vibration. Everything moves according to the Law of Attraction, which states "Like attracts like." In other words, for as long as we carry guilt, hate, resentment, or judgments against others or ourselves, we cannot be attracted to these higher realms. There are no shortcuts to return Home. We have to use our time here on Earth to learn to love everything around us and within us—without conditions, without limitations, and no exclusions. This Love takes no position; it is rising above separation and polarities. This Love is our true essence and as such it is the most powerful basis for our courage.

It is my strong conviction that being born and living in these stormy times is a tremendous privilege, not a curse. I believe that we have consciously chosen to come to this planet at this point of time, not only to help others but mostly because we need these challenges and conditions to grow and wake up to our true divinity.

This is the time for us to demonstrate who we truly are. It may be scary at times, and we may need a lot of courage to face some of the adversities. But, fortunately, we will never have to face them alone. As we know from the scriptures, even in our darkest hours we are not left without help or guidance. We are always in the presence of our spiritual guides, whether we call them God, Christ, prophets, saints, or guardian angels. Just like a competent captain steering the boat safely through the storm, they are here to assist us through every crisis. However, when the tempest is howling around us and is shaking up our life, we often fail to hear their guidance. These are the moments when we need to stop and ground ourselves and open up to their message. For this reason I have created this book.

This book is not only helpful in times of major upheavals, but also in quiet times for reflection and meditation. It contains a large array of empowering insights, quotes, and affirmations that speak to different levels of your soul. Not all of them may be right for you at this particular point in time, but your spiritual guide knows which words have the power of inspiration that you need to hear right now. You can read this book chapter by chapter or open it randomly. Either way, you will come across some particular insights that give you an inner surge of energy, a freeing sensation, the feeling of courage, or a deep peacefulness. It's like an inner voice saying, "Yes, I knew that all the time. But I had forgotten." These physical affirmative sensations are coming directly from your spiritual guide. They are the joy your guide feels when you are reconnecting to your inner wisdom and truth. This is one of the most dramatic ways in which the nonphysical world is communicating its joy with us.

Whenever you have these positive inner sensations, I invite you to stay with these messages and reflect on them before you read on. There may be much more your guardian spirit wants to communicate to you. As you close your eyes and let the words vibrate through you, images, thoughts, and feelings may come up that may give you the specific guidance and solutions that you seek. The result will be renewed courage and strength.

For many years I have tested these quotations in my own life whenever I found myself in the midst of a storm. They have not failed me and neither will they fail you, because the wisdom they contain is the same wisdom that is in all of us.

WHEN EVERYTHING AROUND US SEEMS TO BE TUMBLING DOWN

1

Our material universe is a universe of contrasts, of polarities, of opposites, such as white and black, day and night, good and evil, and so on. When we carefully study all these complementary opposites we will see that they are in perfect balance with each other to ensure the continuation of Creation. One cannot have one without the other; therefore, we cannot have construction without destruction. In the Western world many of us have been brought up with the idea that construction is usually considered "good" and destruction is often seen as "bad." However, in the East both forces are considered equal and necessary for the process of Creation. Every newly built house is a result of an equal amount of destruction of landscape, timber, minerals, resources, and so on. Everything in this universe is in constant rotation of destruction and construction. Every atom is formed and eventually disintegrates before it is formed anew. So does every molecule, every cell, every body, every system, every city, and every civilization. Even planets and stars. Entire galaxies are constantly forming and constantly disintegrating—only to be born new again. Everything is changing and becoming. Nothing ever stands still.

I cannot help but be in awe when I see this perfect universe where every phase of the cycle is fully balanced with its opposite. In his book *A New Concept of the Universe*, Walter Russell expands on Newton's Third Law by stating that "Every action is simultaneously balanced by an equal opposite reaction, and is repeated sequentially in reverse polarity." Every "negative" is immediately counterbalanced by the same amount of "positive." We reach equanimity, inner peace, and clarity when we begin to see that everything happens in absolute balance and perfection and that love is the synchronicity and symmetry of complementary opposites. Once the fire of love has burned away all our attractions and repulsions to the opposites of life, we will see the world not with indifference but with love and compassion. We will then always have the courage to search out the perfection of the underlying order when others cry and lament about the injustices, horrors, sufferings, and cruelties of this world. When we concentrate on the whole, complete, and balanced picture, we won't waste our energy bemoaning the "negative" side of the cycle, such as destruction and losses. To breathe in new fresh air, we have to first breathe out the old air. To create a new world, a new society, a new life, and a new tomorrow, we have to replace the old. And that may mean that certain old structures have to come down first.

What happens when the walls around us tumble? They reveal new horizons and let us look further than we could ever see before. Therefore, the destruction of our inner and outer walls may be the best thing that could happen to us. It may set us free and reawaken in us dreams and aspirations of a new life here or on another level. Have we not been told that this life on Earth is only temporary and we should not build our homes here?

When everything around us is tumbling down we may think it's at its worst. But in truth, it may just be at its very best for us.

There is a right time for everything.
Everything on earth has its special season.
There is a time to be born and a time to die.
There is a time to plant and a time to pull up plants.
There is a time to kill and a time to heal.
There is a time to destroy and a time to build.
There is a time to cry and a time to laugh.
There is a time to be sad and a time to dance.
There is a time to throw away stones and a time
    to gather them.
There is a time to hug and a time not to hug.
There is a time to look for something and a time
    to stop looking for it.
There is a time to keep things and a time
    to throw things away.
There is a time to tear apart and a time to sew together.
There is a time to be silent and a time to speak.
There is a time to love and a time to hate.
There is a time for war and a time for peace.

Ecclesiastes 3:1–8

It was the best of times, it was the worst of times;
it was the age of wisdom, it was the age of foolishness;
it was the epoch of belief, it was the epoch of credulity;
it was the season of light, it was the winter of despair.

Charles Dickens

The will of God is equilibrium.

St. Augustine

Be reconciled
with all opposites
of life

Ayurveda Teaching

If we accept God as perfect, we must admit a perfect universe and cosmic scheme. If, however, we do not accept a belief in a perfect universe, then we have to accept an imperfect Creator.

Henry R. Hamblin

Nor can any evil happen to anyone without it being balanced at once by the Lord, thus by the good.

Emanuel Swedenborg

To achieve inner peace in troubling times we have to stop and see the perfect equilibrium of the "negative" and "positive." The moment we discover this balance in our life and in this entire universe, true inner peace will return.

The darkness and light are both alike to Thee.

Psalm 139.12

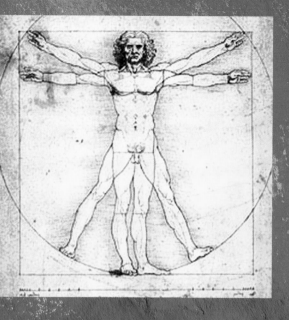

Perfection above me

Perfection below me

Perfection to my right

Perfection to my left

Perfection behind me

Perfection before me

Recognize the simplicity that everything happens in absolute perfection and have the courage to search out the underlying order at any moment of your life.

Instead of spending all our energies on fighting the "bad," we better focus on the truth, which is the perfect balance of all complementary opposites.

There is nothing either good or bad, but thinking makes it so.

William Shakespeare

The life must be a well-balanced life, not lopsided in any manner, to bring contentment...

Edgar Cayce

Nothing occurs by accident and there are
no coincidences. Our lives are divinely designed
for and by each of us to get exactly what we
need to support our own evolutionary process.

There are no errors in life. Even the most difficult
situation is nothing but a lesson in love.

John Demartini

Never give up—even in your darkest hour.
Because your grandest adventure is just
about to begin....

Troubled waters are not here to drown us but to **cleanse** us.

Once, during my years of work in hospice, I had an amazing dream, or perhaps it was a vision, that has always stayed with me. I was led into a circular room that was filled with an incredible, resplendent light. In the center of the room stood an old white-haired man who was translucent and almost seemed to be composed of light itself. He pointed to the wall of the room, which was covered with a collage of pictures. I saw that each picture was a scene from my life—representing both significant and trival events, times of celebration and suffering, achievement, and failure. I observed that each scene had its own shape, and that all of the scenes fit together perfectly, as do the pieces of a jigsaw puzzle. Awestruck, I whispered, "It's all perfect. Everything that has happened has been perfect!" He nodded in agreement. I went on to bemoan, "Oh, if only I had realized this before. I regret all the time I wasted worrying about things and feeling despair. I just didn't..." He placed a finger on my lips to silence me. Again pointing to the collage, he spoke, "Look! Even the worrying was perfect."

Karen Wyatt, M.D.

Life is like the wrong side of a carpet. We see many different colored threads running every which way. They seem to make no sense at all. But one day in this life or thereafter, we will see the right side of the carpet and then we will realize that everything has made a perfect pattern.

No matter what happens to us, there is a divine plan uniquely expressing itself as our individual lives.

Walter Starcke

You are the master of your life if you can honestly say "so what" to anything that happens to you. It shows you are emotionally free of it and can move on. "So what" are two of the most healing words, as they represent a relinquishment of the excuses for why things haven't worked out for you.

The mask of your ignorance is the depth
of your belief in injustice and tragedy.
What the caterpillar calls the end of the world,
the master calls a butterfly.

Richard Bach

As every storm cleanses the earth and the air, so does every storm in our life cleanse us from that which is no longer needed. The stronger the storm, the greater the Love that blows through us.

Our trials and difficulties are not here to break us.
On the contrary, we seek them out to gain wisdom
and to grow. They are treasures in disguise. We
are not in Tribulation but in Transformation.

Our life on Earth is always changing—nothing ever
stays the same and everything comes to an end
—even the most difficult periods in our life.

All material things are merely tools. And if tools
have become useless, or are no longer needed by us,
we have to let them go.

In every tragedy lies the chance
for immense growth.

When everything is crashing down
and collapses, remember that there
is a Force in us that never changes
—ever. It is always stable and present
within ourselves and waiting for us to
call on it.

Difficult and challenging times are empowering
times to reconnect us with our inner guidance
—our Higher Self, with God.

Everything is for the ultimate good—even the
temporary bad.

If we think of ourselves as a raw diamond, we may curse the work of the cutter, grinder, and polisher and may even call them "evil." But without their efforts, our radiant beauty would never be revealed.

WHEN FACING TOUGH SITUATIONS

2

One of my favorite stories in the Bible is the story of Joseph.
Here we have a young boy sold by his own brothers into slavery.
When he is wrongly accused of attempted rape, he is thrown into
prison. But at the end of the story he becomes a powerful and
wealthy man who not only forgives his brothers but also provides
their families with food during the time of famine. This is the
story I would like to remember when all my worldly comforts and
security are threatened or taken away. In spite of how dreadful
it may appear, life will go on and it will all make sense in the
end—but it is not easy to keep this truth in mind in the midst
of the storm.

We often act like someone who is looking at a beautiful tapestry with his nose too close to the weaving. All we see are different colored dots that make no sense at all. Many of them actually scare us, particularly the dark ones. But only when we move a few steps away from the tapestry will we see its beautiful pattern and that all the dots—even the dark ones—make a perfect design, a beautiful picture.

Imagine how the world looks from the perspective of a tiny mouse in a meadow. This little creature can see only a few inches ahead; he doesn't know what is lurking behind the next corner. But an eagle has wings and as he soars higher and higher he not only sees the whole meadow, but the entire land from horizon to horizon. The eagle sees the Big Picture. And if we spread our inner wings we too can see the Big Picture of our life and know that everything makes a perfect pattern. Gratefully will we then accept that there are no coincidences and that everything has a purpose and is designed to be for our best.

Instead of complaining and bemoaning our situation we will then concentrate on the changes we want.

It may require courage to see our difficulty as a blessing and treasure instead of a curse or an obstacle. But once we do, we will be experiencing what we sought out to experience, when it was created for ourselves and by ourselves.

When faced with a difficult situation, ask "I brought this into my life to show me something—what is it? And how can I work with it, in love and in light?" Once we open ourselves up to the message that the difficult situation is trying to tell us, its purpose has been fulfilled. There are no errors in life -- only lessons in love. The question to ask is not "Why me?" but rather "Where and how have I been doing the same thing to myself and others?", "And how has it served me?", and "How can I use it?"

John Demartini

Anything that we do not **love** keeps us imprisoned.

The circumstances on Earth are not the ultimate.
The ultimate is the attitude we have towards
such circumstances.

Things are never bad.
It's the way we think about them.

Epictetus

Not the situation disturbs us but our opinion of the
situation.

Seneca

It is not the load that weights us down—
it's the way we carry it.

The outcome
of an event is
much less significant
than what I become
through the
experience.

There is no such thing
as a problem without a
gift for you in its hands.
You seek problems
because you need
their gifts.

Richard Bach

A problem always ceases to exist the moment we give all our concentration to the solution.

We are all blessed with an internal guiding system that will lead us to the right people, circumstances, and places if we are willing to listen.

Why do bad things happen to good people? Because we fail to see the big picture and the underlying order of everything.
Ultimately, there are no bad things and no good things. There are only consequences of choices made.

What are you afraid of?
You can only meet what is yours and what will serve you.
I see the day when you will bless the sufferings
that have taught you to become who you truly are.

German Proverb

Wise men count their blessings; fools their problems.

For what is perfect living? Dealing with that
which is before us by making the highest choices
to aid our soul and for the benefit of all.

No matter how much the ignorant
will complain and disagree—
life is a succession of
perfect moments.

Only our ego knows fear
and worries because it
identifies with our body.
Let us become the observer,
observing our ego experiencing
the fear.

I am not my troubles,
I am not the experience.
I am the experiencer.
I am the observer.

Don't take yourself so serious.

Use your imagination and make your difficulties smaller, make them funny, give them a silly-sounding voice, bright colors, or dots and shapes. You are the master of your life. Don't let your troubles master you.

HOW TO DEAL WITH DIFFICULT PEOPLE

3

I have great respect for political activists who put their hearts and lives on the line to make a change in the world. But it has always amazed me that so many of the antiwar protesters have angry and aggressive natures that cause them to occasionally express their views in highly destructive actions during their demonstrations.

It was only after I studied the law of projections that this seeming contradiction made total sense to me. The Law of Projection is a mental law of the mind. It says that whatever we project on the screen of our mind we perceive in the world around us. In other words, whatever we see "inwardly" determines what we see "outside" of ourselves. If I perceive hate and anger within me, I notice a lot of hate and anger around me. If I see love in me, I will also see love outside of me— whatever is in me determines what I see in the world around me. In his book *The Power of Now,* Eckart Tolle calls the world within us the Primary Reality and the world outside of us the Secondary Reality. The Primary Reality determines how we experience the Secondary Reality.

46

The world around us reflects to us who we are, what we judge, what we fear, and all our beliefs. This applies particularly to people who are "pushing our buttons." They mirror to us beliefs, behavior patterns, attitudes, or character traits that we either have overtly or secretly repressed. That's why this law is also called the "You spot it—you got it!" law.

We are what we see in others. People who give us emotional charges are reflecting a charge we have against ourselves. It can go even so far that a person who is physically hurting us is also reflecting a hurt that we have inflicted inwardly to ourselves. Whatever people outwardly do unto us we have been doing inwardly to ourselves; in other words, people are expressing what we are repressing. If we inwardly attack, push, resist, we feel outwardly attacked, pushed, or resisted by others.

Therefore, it would make more sense to be grateful to the people who push our buttons. They offer a valuable gift to us as they make us aware of who we are and what we still have to clear up within ourselves. But being grateful to them does not mean we have to endure or tolerate their abusive behavior. The fastest way to change them is to change ourselves.

47

Anything that we don't like or resent we have created on some level of our consciousness. If we keep blaming others and circumstances, we disempower ourselves. Only by taking full responsibility to whatever happens to us do we find the power to change it.

When we see ourselves as victims, we think only about killing the messenger, and end up missing the message.

No one victimizes us: they just reflect us. Anything that we suppress or disown we send out as vibration and will attract it into our life in one form or another. So, through marriage, business partnership, friends, etc., we are attracting our "disowned" parts. What we don't like or ignore in ourselves we keep attracting until we learn the message it contains.

John Demartini

Attacks are not against us.
They are cries for love,
calls for attention,
or pleas for help.

A man only begins to be a man when he ceases to whine
and revile, and commences to search for the hidden justice
which regulates his life.

James Allen

There are no victims and no villains. The person who is persecuting us is merely playing out an agreement made on a whole different level so that we might learn unconditional, unlimited, and all-inclusive Love.

Be deeply grateful for the person who has been teaching us a hard lesson. It's not easy for a soul to come into this life and commit "horrendous" acts or crimes so that we will wake up and learn our lessons.

We are not victims of villains or circumstances, but victims of our own perception.

Shakespeare observed that "All the world is a stage, and all the men and women merely players. They have their exits and entrances; each man in his time plays many parts." Therefore, let us always see and concentrate on the complete innocence behind the mask of the actor. That is how God sees us.

51

Every person we meet is an expression of **God.**
Therefore, we can never overestimate the value
of another human being.

Do not try to see the "best" in anyone—for that is judgment
of the ego. You are here to perceive Truth, which is beyond
all concepts of best or worst. Look beyond all appearances
and judgments and see as God sees.

Irrespective of
what we think about
our neighbor and his action,
God's adoration for him will
never cease nor change.

When looking at
another person,
don't look at
their gender, race, or appearance.
Simply look at their wings.
Everyone is an angel in disguise
—including you!

The only forgiveness we can ever need to do is the forgiving of ourselves for not having seen the other person as perfect and divine. The problem is never out there with the other person, but exists only within us as misperception. Whatever we condemn in others we have condemned in ourselves, repressed, denied, and then projected onto others.

Understanding everything
means forgiving
everything.

He who does not forgive only holds himself prisoner.

Do not cry for "Justice"
because justice means
that we, essentially,
want something "bad"
to happen to another
because something
"bad" has happened to us.
But God is Love, and Love does not punish nor
want anything "bad" to happen to anyone.

The actual Truth never requires forgiveness.

We eventually have to love everyone and everything because it is all God. Loving takes no energy at all. It is what our soul longs for. It is the opposite that drains us.

Be kind, for everyone you meet is fighting a harder battle.
Plato

Everyone functions to their own best ability at any given moment. No one does less than their own best—ever. Therefore, never expect anything from others that they are unable to give.

Kindness towards others and oneself is a very powerful transformation force.

Every enemy ceases to exist once we have listened to their story.

$$1 + 1 = 1$$

"Love Thy Neighbor as Thyself" is meant literally, because thy neighbor is yourself. There is no separation between him and yourself. Never be fooled by the illusion of separation. Like the fingers on one hand we are all One. Always.

WHEN WE ARE SCARED ABOUT THE FUTURE

4

Embracing uncertainties is something most of us are not comfortable with, particularly in times of drastic changes. We do everything to obtain and maintain certainty in our lives to buffer us from any winds of change. We sign up for things such as marriage licenses and insurance policies to feel "secure." This deep desire for certainty comes from our ego, which can only deal with the known, the past. The ego wants certainty on its own terms, but these terms are all fallacies.

It is our soul that wants to evolve, grow, and experience life. And for this our soul needs change as much as our lungs need air to breathe. Our soul has consciously chosen to come to this world at this particular time because of all the changes that are upon us. We did not come to hide and hold onto the old. We are here to experience, explore—and also enjoy—all the exhilarating uncertainties that are coming our way. As every toddler enjoys his or her first own successful steps, so can we find pleasure from observing our own growth process even in the worst of times.

Uncertainty is the basis of life because life is change. It is the Gift from God and it is up to us to revel in it and rejoice at every turn. He who is not afraid of uncertainties will walk free in the face of all adversities.

Let us embrace uncertainties as an essential ingredient of our experience of every day. The more uncertainty, the more joy in our life. In uncertainty there is pure creativity and freedom. The fun, the excitement, the adventure, and mystery in life are always in taking some risks. At any moment in our life we are standing on the threshold of the long-sought-after new beginning.

Don't call it uncertainties—call it wonder.
Don't call it insecurity—call it freedom.

Osho

Nietzsche once said, you must have uncertainty and chaos
within you to give birth to a dancing star. If you are certain,
then you are a prisoner of the known. There's nothing to do;
there's nothing to teach you. Uncertainty opens you up to the
field of infinite possibilities, which is fresh and ever new.
And there is nothing more important than embracing
the wisdom of uncertainty, because when you do,
you psychologically unburden yourself. Your certainties
are what imprison you in the past—because what's the
known, but the past. It's the prison of past conditioning.

Deepak Chopra

The only difference between the rut and the grave
is the depth.

Embrace all uncertainties of the future to become free, strong, and alive!

Change, rather than being a destructive force, is a creative and life-enriching force. It stimulates us to reach our highest potential. What we really should fear is if our lives do not change enough.

The goal of life is freedom. Freedom is the letting go of the known.

Let us not be tied to the comforts of yesterday. Possessions, status, circle of friends, and more may have to change to make us "lighter" so that we are attracted to higher realms for the enjoyment and growth of our soul.

A ship in harbor
is safe, but that
is not what ships
are built for.

John A. Shedd

Feel the power of the eternal YES. Live it and be it with every word, thought, and action. YES is the Creative Force of the Universe. The word NO is contrary to reality and is the source of all suffering.

By seeing the positive in every negative we can move on. Instead of resisting what is, we accept it and can use the energy to make the change we want.

Surrender to whatever the moment brings.

Surrender the desire to control everything to God with humility. The act of humility open us up to guidance, strength, and love.

Invoke the fullness that you are by saying repeatedly the words "I AM." Feel them vibrate through your body. Feel your connection with God's energy and let it strengthen you. Feel the release of your fears and anxieties.

Take therefore no thought for the morrow: for the morrow shall take thought for the things of itself.

Matthew 6:34

If we did the things we are capable of doing, we would literally astound ourselves.

Thomas Alva Edison

Do not be too timid and squeamish about your actions. All life is an experiment. The more experiments you make the better. What if they are a little course, and you may get your coat soiled or torn? What if you do fail, and get fairly rolled in the dirt once or twice. Up again, you shall never be so afraid of a tumble.

Ralph Waldo Emerson

The amount of courage determines how grand our life will be.

To live without fear we must fully understand and appreciate that every situation and every outcome is nothing but perfect—including the outcome we seem to fear most, which is death. Except, there is no death. We merely make a transition into the non-physical. Our life continues and death is the door to a new adventure. For too long we have spent much energy in fearing death. If we now accept the true nature of death, these energies will then charge us with life!

Only cowards hate change, because they wish to keep on living and thinking in their customary ways. But the brave ones set fire to that which is old and continue onward.

The true warrior neither seeks nor flees from death.
He knows that death does not exist.
Spirit is eternal and always has been.

Steps

As every flower fades and as all youth
Departs, so life at every stage,
So every virtue, so our grasp of truth
Blooms in its day and may not last forever.
Since life may summon us at every age
Be ready, heart, for parting, new endeavor,
Be ready bravely and without remorse
To find new light that old ties cannot give.
In all beginnings dwells a magic force
For guarding us and helping us to live.

Serenely let us move to distant places
And let no sentiments of home detain us.
The Cosmic Spirit seeks not to restrain us
But lifts us stage by stage to wider spaces.
If we accept a home of our own making,
Familiar habit makes for indolence.
We must prepare for parting and leave-taking
Or else remain the slaves of permanence.

Even the hour of our death may send
Us speeding on to fresh and newer spaces,
And life may summon us to newer races.
So be it, heart: bid farewell without end.

Hermann Hesse

WHEN FEAR AND WORRY OVERTAKE

We are all familiar with the "negative" side of fear—the contracting, stifling, and sometimes paralyzing emotion. But—like everything— fear also has a "positive" side that we need to keep in mind when the emotion of fear tries to overpower us.

I am thinking of my life and home in Africa when increasing civil unrest and the potential of a bloody war forced me to leave all that was dear and familiar to me behind. Yes, it was fear that drove me away and into a new life full of adventure. I lived in many countries and cultures; I started a new and rewarding career that takes me all over the world; I married a wonderful woman and now live close to one of the most exciting cities in the world. All this because I was "afraid."

The positive side of fear is a gift to motivate us to go where we want to go or ought to be. It gets us out of our comfort zones and helps us to do our best in a new situation. It is no coincidence that the sensation of fear is identical to the one we have when we are excited. It is only after we have filtered this body sensation through our mind and analyzed it that we call it either negative or positive. We either respond with "Oh, no!" or respond in an excited way with "Oh, great!" It's the same energy. A typical example is a ride on a roller coaster. For one person this may be the most frightening experience in the world and for another it is total exhilaration. Same feeling—different interpretations.

With this understanding that we can change our attitude toward fear, we can begin calling our fears *adventures*! Then we will not deprive ourselves of its exciting stirring sensation. By our accepting and loving it, fear will fulfill its true role for us: it will propel us forward! Someone once said: F.E.A.R. stands for Feeling Excited And Ready!

With this new understanding of fear, it is much easier for us to replace the negative side of fear with faith in God.

When we see the divine order—the underlying perfection and balance in everything—our fears will disappear.

As light dispels darkness, so does love dispel fear. Learn to love every aspect of that which you fear and you have conquered fear. If you cannot love it, at least appreciate its value, for everything has its purpose for the benefit of your growth.

To understand fear, you must understand thought. Thought is time. Without thought, there is no fear. Without time, there is no fear. Because we have time and because we have thought, there is fear. If we are faced with something factual, there is no fear. If you are going to die the next instant, then you accept it, there is no fear. But if you say that you are going to die the day after tomorrow, then you have forty-eight hours to worry about it, to get sick about it. So time is fear; thought is fear. And the ending of thought, the ending of time, is the ending of fear.

Krishnamurti

Fear contracts the body and love expands it.
By conciously breathing deeply and slowly we
can imagine filling our body with love, and thus
expanding it.

We only fear when we forget
who walks beside us.

Fear thou not:
for I am with thee:
be not dismayed;
for I am thy God:
I will strengthen thee:
yea, I will help thee.

Isaiah 41:10

The Lord is my light and my salvation;
whom shall I fear?
The Lord is the strength of my life;
of whom shall I be afraid?

Psalm 27:1

Fear arises from lack of awareness of
God's omnipresence in us. Therefore,
whenever the slightest hint of fear arises,
say "Oh, God, stand by me. I need thee."

But thou, O Lord, art a shield for me;
my glory, and the lifter up of mine head.
I cried unto the Lord with my voice,
and he heard me out of his holy hill, Selah.
I laid me down and sleep: I awake again,
for the Lord sustains me.
I will not be afraid.

Psalm 3:3–6

The Lord is my shepherd; I shall not want.

He maketh me to lie down in green pastures:

he leadeth me beside the still waters.

He restoreth my soul: he leadeth me in the

path of righteousness for his name's sake.

Yea, though I walk through the valley of the

shadow of death, I will fear no evil:

for thou art with me: thy rod and thy staff

they comfort me.

Though preparest a table before me in the

presence of mine enemies: thou anointest

my head with oil; my cup runneth over.

Surely goodness and mercy shall follow me
all the days of my life: and I will dwell in the
house of the LORD forever.

Psalm 23

How would you feel if you had no fear?
Feel like that.
How would you behave toward other people
if you realized their powerlessness to hurt you?
Behave like that.
How would you react to so-called misfortune
if you saw its inability to bother you?
React like that.
How would you think toward yourself if you
knew you were really all right?
Think like that.

Vernon Howard

Feel courageous in spirit, then fear will
lose its power!

Waste no time with worry or fear. Simply ask
"What needs to be done next?" and your
energy goes into the solution instead of the
problem.

Many of our fears are tissue paper-thin, and a single courageous step would carry us through them.

Brendan Francis

All our negative emotions are basically the fear of letting go.

Anger is fear. Every angry person is a frightened one, dreading some potential loss.

Let us not be afraid of loss. Loss is an illusion, for nothing ever gets lost in the universe. It only changes form. Therefore, we cannot lose anything. It is always with us—just in another form. We may lose the warmth of summer, but we gain the harvest and beauty of autumn. We may lose the strength of youth, but we gain the wisdom of age.

There is no fear nor worry
for those who know
how to stay in the
Here and Now

Celebrate each
moment as new
and unique.

WHEN FAITH IS AT ITS LOWEST

6

Faith is something that nobody can give us. We all have to develop it for ourselves. Faith is like the first little baby steps that we took without knowing for sure that we would be successful. But once we saw that we could manage the first few steps, our faith grew and grew and soon no obstacle could stop us in our delight in walking, running, or racing.

In his book *Words I Have Lived By,* Norman Vincent Peale writes, "When real faith grips you, you develop a mind-set that looks for the best in everything, refuses to give up, finds a way around (or through) every obstacle, and presses on to victory."

But how do we maintain a strong faith when everything around us seems to be tumbling down? The mere understanding that in the end all these changes will be for the best for everyone may not be enough to give us the inner peace that faith can offer. It requires more than that. It requires the strengthening of our inner connection with God and all the heavenly helpers who are standing by our side to guide us through the difficulties. Prayers, meditations, inner reflections, words of inspiration, and songs are also practical tools to bring us closer to God and our spiritual guides.

Even if we don't always see the underlying perfection of everything, let us be grateful in advance for whatever comes. Let the spirit of thanksgiving flood our whole being with its healing warmth.

When everything around us is falling apart,
let us go within in silence and be guided
by the One Who dwells within us.

Through prayer we touch the highest in ourselves,
touch God, and connect to Love and open ourselves
to guidance.

A powerful way to pray is to pray alone and aloud.
Spiritual songs and hymns can fill the soul with strength
and peace.

Dear God, I ask now that only what is the
highest and best for all concerned will happen.
And I leave it to You to know and to decide
what that is. Amen

We do not pray to get something.
We pray to *become* something.

You cannot fall deeper
than into the hands of God.

For with God nothing
shall be impossible.

Luke 1:37

Place all your troubles on the
altar of God. He will transform
them into love, for nothing is
too big for God.

In whatever situation we find
ourselves, we are never forgotten
or alone. God is always with us
because we are part of God.

Be still, and know that I am God.

Psalm 46:10

What could possibly be more important than our inner connection with God? The only place for renewal of our strength is within us when we commune with God. Here is the ever-flowing source of courage and ideas for action.

God's Love is the Love that heals.

Have the courage to face your painful feeling—whether
it be fear, worry, frustration, anger, or whatever else. Sit
down in a comfortable chair and give all your attention
to this feeling. Do it without any judgment or the need to
change it. Observe where you are experiencing this feeling
in your body and its specific sensations. For the next few
minutes explore the feeling and be totally present with it
without analyzing or judging it.

Now breath into this feeling and make it even bigger,
magnify it, intensify it, and allow it to express itself in
your body even further. Do this for a few minutes.

Finally, give that feeling all the love you are capable of.
Love it, love it, love it, and observe how the feeling
vanishes when bathed in unlimited, unconditional, and
all-inclusive Love.

But they that wait upon the Lord
shall renew their strength;
they shall mount up with wings as eagles;
they shall run, and not be weary;
and they shall walk, and not faint.

Isaiah 40:31

Today is the tomorrow you were worried
about yesterday.

Do not be afraid of tomorrow,
for God is already there.

I will go before you
and make the crooked
places straight.

Isaiah 45:2

93

We all have **guardian angels** at our side. They love
to help us release our fears and heal our relationship
with ourselves, with others, and with the planet. But
they do not push their help onto us.
We have to ask for their help.

Wrap yourself
in the wings of
your angel.

Let us always be open to the guidance and help offered by our guardian angels, as they are of a higher frequency, and thus are more in tune with the Divine.

Being of service is the greatest joy for our spiritual guardians.

Gratefulness for troubled times lets us see the opportunity to do something about it.

Gratefulness is the fastest form of healing. What we resist, persists. What we are grateful for can then serve us, as it was meant to.

Thanksgiving is not just a reactionary emotion; it is a causative energy. It is an effective key by which anyone may meet life as a powerful conqueror.

Eric Butterworth

The mind cannot be
thankful and worrying
at the same time.

Even if we don't always see the underlying perfection
of everything, let us be grateful in advance for whatever
comes. Let the spirit of thanksgiving flood our whole
being with its healing warmth.

WHEN WE SUFFER
7

When I was growing up I had a hard time understanding why God would allow so much pain and suffering in the world, but with the years I began to see that pain and sufferings are powerful tools to remind us of our own highest ideals whenever we have wandered away from them. The grace of God gives us many warning signals before most pain begins, but our human nature often prefers to ignore them. Therefore, the Christian thinker C. S. Lewis calls pain "God's megaphone to rouse the deaf world."

It also helped me to grasp the difference between pain and suffering. Pain is the physical experience, whereas suffering is the perception or judgment that we have about this experience as well as its anticipation and memory. For instance, if we can find a purpose in the pain, we can bear virtually any pain. A typical example is the case of childbirth. A *New York Times* report says that "in quantitative ratings of pain severity, the pain of a first labor exceeds cancer pain by a considerable margin and falls just shy of the pain of a limb amputation sans anesthesia." But in spite of these extreme pains, many women accept these torments again and again and even decline any form of anesthesia or painkillers during the childbearing process. Nietzsche put it so well when he said, "He who has a why can endure any how."

In most cases the suffering of anticipated or past pain is far more severe than the actual pain. The reason is quite simple: Physical pain can be experienced only in the very short span of the present moment. It cannot be experienced in the past nor in the future. But with our judgment of the pain that we call suffering, we can linger in the past or the future for as long as we "enjoy" it. In other words, we may not be able to totally avoid pain, but we can choose if, how, and how long we wish to suffer. Suffering is always a choice.

We suffer because we are convinced that our life, people, and situations should be different than what they are. With suffering we try to avoid the reality of life and ignore that everything is here to serve us for our highest good.

Suffering is the ego's tool to obstruct our view of reality. It allows us to feel hurt or insulted and blame others for our situation. But every time we judge or condemn anything, we are denying God and the underlying divine order of everything.

But he who is grieved and laments demonstrates that he is undergoing some hardship and suffering, and lacks some goodness; he is like a heretic, who denies God's omnipresence. For if he would truly believe, he would realize that in the light of the King's countenance there is life, and strength and joy are in His place, so that he indeed lacks nothing.

From the Tanja

We are the only ones who can do anything about our life experience. Nobody else can contain their behavior so that we will feel better—we are the only ones who have that power.

The more things go "wrong" in our life, the more evidence we have of our incredible power because we are always creating our own reality. If we can create "wrong," we can most certainly also create "right."

If we think we cannot love something, we can ask our inner guidance to show us the value of it. We can then learn to appreciate and value it. This includes everything that makes us suffer.

If you are pained by any external thing, it is not this thing that disturbs you, but your own judgement about it. It is in your power to erase this judgement now. If anything in your own nature gives you pain, you are the one who hinders you from correcting your opinion.

Marcus Aurelius

Much of our suffering is merely resistance to accepting what is.

The danger with suffering is that we can get too attached to it when we begin to identify with our troubles, afflictions, and misery. But we are none of this. We are merely indulging in self-pity. Meanwhile, the entire universe is waiting for us to get off our self-pity-potty.

Change is inevitable—suffering is optional.

When getting caught up in our tragedies, let us remember that the only difference between tragedy and comedy is time. With time, every tragedy becomes comedy.

The greatest tragedy is suffering
the pain without learning the lesson.

Goethe

The tragedies of life are
nothing else but lessons of
unconditional, unlimited, and
all-inclusive Love. And they
will be repeated over and
over again until we learn
the lesson.

We are not our body and we are not our sickness.
Neither are we our lacks and misfortunes.
These are merely our experiences.
There is a distinction and separation
between the experience and the
observer of the experience.
We are the observer—
never the experience.

Diseases can be our spiritual flat tires—
disruptions in our lives that seem to
be disasters at the time but end by
redirecting our lives in a meaningful
way.

Bernie Siegel, M.D.

Let us be thankful in advance for the good
that is going to happen in and through us
as a result of what we are experiencing.

I consider that the sufferings of this present time are not worth comparing with the glory that is to be revealed to us.

Romans 8:18

WHAT IS OUR TASK IN THESE DIFFICULT TIMES?

When I was a lot younger, I dreamed of retiring one day to a little beach house on some forgotten island and letting the world pass me by. But with age all desires for retirement have vanished and are replaced with the strong desire of fulfilling my purpose. I'd rather like to end like a candle burning on both ends than never having explored my full potential.

It is my conviction that many of us are here on Earth at precisely this moment because our talents and services are needed in these difficult times. We all have a different purpose to fulfill, and if we listen to our inner guidance, we will be shown where and how we can be of optimal use. The number of people who may benefit from our help is unimportant because our work is not judged by quantity. All we are asked is to show up and to live up to our own highest ideals in every situation and see the love in everything and everyone.

Having lived in a mystical community for many years, I have found great benefit in having been surrounded by like-minded people. This is particularly true for very challenging times when people who are focused and know that they have a purpose to fulfill are rare—but there are ways to find such people. Many towns and neighborhoods have prayer circles or wisdom circles where friends with similiar views can be found—and if not, start one yourself.

It was our choice to come to this planet at this time, and one of our most important tasks is to heal. First, heal ourselves and then others. Heal, heal, heal wherever we go, wherever we are. Most importantly, it is the healing of our own perception until we see that everything is according to the Grand Organizing Design.

Those of us who lived through the concentration camps can remember very clearly the men and women who walked through the huts comforting those in need and giving away their last piece of bread. They may have been few in numbers but they are a testimony to the possibilities of the human spirit.

Victor Frankl

Only because we think we're not
perfect doesn't mean we are not
an ambassador of the Light.
Martin Luther King Jr., Gandhi, Mother
Theresa, and many others were
all bright and healing lights in spite
of their human imperfections.

Do not wait for leaders;
do it alone, person to person.

Mother Theresa

Courage is the realization and execution of individual capacities to the betterment of tomorrow. Dare to use your talents and utilize them for the good of all.

Jack van Hulst

We are God's hands and feet here on Earth.

When you feel sad for others, wanting to alleviate their suffering, remember that nothing happens randomly. It is more like a carefully orchestrated play in which many have chosen to play very dramatic roles, in full awareness of their part in the whole. But observe it with compassion and not with indifference.

Whatever our tasks may be, we must not allow any pessimism as to the ultimate future of mankind. Abraham Lincoln and Winston Churchill battled depression, but they saw a better future where others saw doom.

Never doubt that a small group of thoughtful, committed citizens can change the world. Indeed, it's the only thing that ever has.

Margaret Mead

Blessed be God...
who comforts us in all our affliction,
so that we may be able to comfort those
who are in any affliction.

2 Corinthians 1:3,4

Hold on to your vision of a new life for yourself and the whole world. Feel this vision with every fiber of your being. Feel it as if you already have achieved it.

Celebrate life—
even in the midst of a storm.
Bring joy and love because you
are joy and love!

The surest way to experience what we want for ourselves is helping others to achieve it. If we want peace, love, and attention, we must first give it to others and it will be ours by the simple act of giving it away. The same applies to courage. If we help others to become courageous, we become courageous. What we give we become.

Our heart always tells us if we are "on track": An expanding heart means that we are living up to our highest goals; a contracting heart means we are run by our ego, our little self.

117

As the sun must shine to be the sun,
so must we love to be **Love**.

True **compassion** can
only come when we
perceive all of
Creation as
our Self.

The well-being of ourselves
and the well-being of others
are, in fact, one and the same.

When everyone is confused by the illusions and distortions around us, we have to strive to see the underlying divine order. There is perfection and balance in everything. Stay focused and see the glory of the process—even in the midst of tragedy and chaos.

Never let the problems overwhelm you. Don't get paralyzed. Start somewhere, anywhere, with just the smallest gesture of kindness or compassion, and you have made a dent for the good in the universe.

It may seem that we have no control over the macrocosm but we have always full control over our own microcosm and that is where we have to do our work.

Jack van Hulst

IN CONCLUSION

We are living in challenging times of unprecedented and momentous changes and we need to remind ourselves that it is a privilege to be here at this moment in time. We have "enrolled" in this lifetime because we carry within us every needed resource, skill, strength, and guidance to face any obstacle that presents itself to us individually and collectively.

By consciously communicating with God—the only Power there is—we can muster all the courage required and see the hidden divine order in everything. What once was a disaster now turns into a miracle that sets us free. Every crisis, problem, or hurdle becomes an adventure and a breakthrough to freedom and spiritual growth.

An exciting time of profound beginnings is upon us and our future will be glorious. Whatever happens to us we shall emerge triumphantly. It is impossible for us to fail because any mistake or detour is just another way of learning to love.

This is not just a time for courageous living but most of all a time for courageous loving. Being part of God, our capacity for loving is infinite. By bringing love and light to others we can truly lighten up this planet.

Blessings,
Hans

ACKNOWLEDGMENTS

James Allen: "As A Man Thinketh," The Peter Pauper Press, New York.

Richard Bach: "Illusions" by Richard Bach, Dell Books, Random House and "Messiah's Handbook" by Richard Bach, Hampton Roads Publishing Co., Inc.

Eric Butterworth: Copyright 2001 by Eric Butterworth. Used by permission of Unity Village, MO *www.unityonline.org*

Edgar Cayce: Edgar Cayce Readings, Copyright 1971, 1993, 2004 by the Edgar Cayce Foundation. Used by permission.

Deepak Chopra: "Sacred Love" Interview with Michael Toms, Copyright 2003 New Dimensions Foundation.

Dr. John Demartini: *www.drmartini.com*

Victor Frankl: "Man's Search for Meaning" by Victor Frankl. Pocket Books, Copyright 1984 Victor Frankl.

Hermann Hesse: "Stages" from THE GLASS BEAD GAME by Hermann Hesse, English language translation by Richard and Clara Winston. Copyright 1997 by Henry Holt and Company. First published in the United States in 1969. Reprinted by permission of Henry Holt and Company, LLC.

Vernon Howard: "Mystic Path to Cosmic Power," by Vernon Howard, Copyright 1999, New Life Foundation, Pine, AZ.

Krishnamurti: "The Collected Works" by Krishnamurti, Vol. 12, p. 303, Copyright 1992 Krishnamurti Foundation of America, *www.kfa.org*

Lynne McTaggart: "The Field" by Lynne McTaggart, published by HarperCollins Publishers, New York, Copyright 2002 by Lynne McTaggart.

Osho: "Courage. The Joy of Living Dangerously," Copyright 1999 by Osho International Foundation. St. Martin's Griffin, New York.

Walter Russell: "The Secret of Light" by Walter Russell, Copyright 1994 by the University of Science and Philosophy.

Emanuel Swedenborg: "Spiritual Experiences 2448," Copyright: Swedenborg Foundation.

Walter Starke: "The Third Appearance" by Walter Starke. Copyright 2004 by Walter Starke, Guadalupe Press, Boerne, TX.

Karen M. Wyatt, M.D.: "Conscious & Healing: Integral Approaches to Mind-Body Medicine," edited by Marilyn Schlitz and Tina Amorok with Marc S. Micozzi, Copyright 2005, Elsevier Inc., St. Louis, Missouri, pp. 217–218.

Special thanks and acknowledgment go to:
Marcus Aurelius, Cicero, Charles Dickens, Thomas Alva Edison, Ralph Waldo Emerson, Epictetus, Victor Frankl, Johann Wolfgang von Goethe, Peter J. Daniels, Brendan Francis, Stephane Janson, Henry R. Hamblin, Margaret Mead, Mother Teresa, Plato, William Shakespeare, Seneca, John A. Shedd, Dr. Bernie Siegel, M.D., St. Augustine, Jack van Hulst, the prophets, the psalmists, the apostles, Mr. & Mrs. Anonymous, and many, many more.

Hans Wilhelm is the author and illustrator of the national best-seller *I'll Always Love You*. He has written and illustrated more than 180 books for young and old with 35 million copies in print. Many of his stories have become successful animated television series.

His books have been translated into more than 20 languages and have won numerous international honors and awards. His book *What Does God Do?* received the Gold Medallion by the Evangelical Christian Publishers Association.

As a noted speaker, Hans Wilhelm has been inspiring audiences around the world with the spiritual and life-affirming concepts that he shares in many of his books.

Hans Wilhelm lives with his artist wife,
Judy Henderson, in Weston, Connecticut.

His Web site: *www.hanswilhelm.com*